WORDS
TO THE
WISE

A COLLECTION OF AFRICAN PROVERBS

WORDS
TO THE
WISE

A COLLECTION OF AFRICAN PROVERBS

Compiled by Julia Stewart

SPEARHEAD

First published in 2003 in Southern Africa by Spearhead,
an imprint of New Africa Books (Pty) Ltd,
99 Garfield Road, Claremont 7700, South Africa

Copyright © 2003 by Julia Stewart

ISBN 0-86486-640-2

All rights reserved. No part of this publication may be
reproduced, stored in a retrieval system, or transmitted in any
form or by any means, electronic, mechanical, photocopying,
recording or otherwise, without the prior written permission
of the publishers.

Typeset in 12 pt Bembo
Cover design by Odette Marais
Printed in South Africa by Creda Communications

Many thanks to Molly Versfeld for supplying the African
images used on the cover and in the text, from copyright-
free design books.

To the wise you tell proverbs, not just words.

GHANA

Leave the handling of the gun to the hunter.

ANGOLA

Ability is wealth.

SWAHILI OF EAST AFRICA

If you can walk you can dance;
if you can talk you can sing.

ZIMBABWE

Stretch your legs the length of your bed.

SWAHILI OF EAST AFRICA

Obedience is better than ability.

PEDI OF SOUTH AFRICA

A dancer cannot know whether he dances well.

BURKINA FASO

If you do not cry out, you will die unheard.

SWAZI OF SOUTH AFRICA AND SWAZILAND

When deeds speak, words are naught.

NDEBELE OF ZIMBABWE AND SOUTH AFRICA

If a snake comes into your house do not
waste time asking where the snake came from,
kill it first and ask questions afterwards.

UGANDA

Good actions are more nourishing
to youth than words.

NORTH AFRICA

A man's deeds are of greater importance
than the facts of his birth.

MAASAI OF KENYA AND TANZANIA

Flowing water makes stagnant water move.

SOMALIA

Where you will sit when you are old
shows where you stood in youth.

YORUBA OF NIGERIA

ADVICE

A man who takes advice,
is still a man who acts of his own free will.

NIGERIA

There is no such thing as a bad king,
only bad counsellors.

AKAN OF GHANA

A person who won't take advice,
gets knowledge when trouble overtakes him.

ZULU OF SOUTH AFRICA

He who fills his head with other people's words
will find no place where he may put his own.

MOROCCO

ADVICE

The fly that has no one to advise it,
follows the corpse into the grave.

NIGERIA

AGE

Old age does not announce itself.

ZULU OF SOUTH AFRICA

An old pot makes water sweet and quickly boils.

OROMO OF ETHIOPIA AND KENYA

There is no difference
between growing old and living.

KIKUYU OF KENYA

Man is like palm wine;
when young sweet, but without strength,
but in age, strong and harsh.

CONGOLESE

ANCESTRY

If we stand tall it is because we stand
on the backs of those who came before us.

YORUBA OF NIGERIA

Go back and fetch what was left behind.

AKAN OF GHANA

However far the stream flows,
it never forgets its source.

YORUBA OF NIGERIA

ANGER

A stone thrown in anger never kills a bird.

YORUBA OF NIGERIA

Anger without power is a blow already.

EGYPT

One does not become so mad at one's head
that one wears one's hat on one's buttocks.

YORUBA OF NIGERIA

AUTHORITY

Even if you know many things,
do not argue with the judge.

ETHIOPIA

It is better to be loved than feared.

SENEGAL

Women have no chiefs.

ACHOLI OF UGANDA

 BEAUTY

A woman is like a merino sheep:
her beauty is judged by her backside.

SOTHO OF LESOTHO AND SOUTH AFRICA

Beauty is not eaten.

KIKUYU OF KENYA

If Miss-this-year is pretty,
Miss-next-year is prettier.

HAUSA OF NIGER AND NIGERIA

12

When he is squandering his gold,
he says his scales are out of order.

AKAN OF GHANA

Those who are absent are always wrong.

CONGOLESE

When one person on the street
kills a dog, the whole street is called
'the street of dog killers.'

NIGERIA

When the ape cannot reach the banana
with its hand, he says it is sour.

BAMBARA OF MALI

It isn't the king who kills you,
it's his court.

RWANDA

One does not become great
by claiming greatness.

XHOSA OF SOUTH AFRICA

If you should become rich,
dance in the house.

NYANJA OF MALAWI AND ZAMBIA

Almost is not eaten.

ZULU OF SOUTH AFRICA

Boasting and a male
cannot be separated.

MAASAI OF KENYA AND TANZANIA

A good thing sells itself;
a bad thing advertises itself for sale.

SWAHILI OF EAST AFRICA

BUSINESS

One who proposes an exchange
knows which is the better.

ETHIOPIA

Love me as if I were your brother
but do your accounts with me
as if I were your enemy.

TUNISIA

CAUTION

Caution is not cowardice;
even the ants march armed.

BAGANDA OF UGANDA

If the tiger sits, do not think it is out of respect.

NILOTIC

He who does not shave you does not cut you.

SOMALIA

15

The sun never sets without fresh news.

ZULU OF SOUTH AFRICA

The world has come to a pretty pass
when an egg drops into an earthen pot
and it is the pot that breaks.

YORUBA OF NIGERIA

We no longer grind with old stones.

ZULU OF SOUTH AFRICA

A new thing is a source of joy
even if that thing be a sore.

SWAHILI OF EAST AFRICA

When the music changes, so does the dance.

HAUSA OF NIGER AND NIGERIA

Kamau who is white becomes black.

KIKUYU OF KENYA

meaning 'there is nothing constant in this world'

16

Of all men, three are the worst:
He who does not patch up his clothes,
He who is irresolute, and
He who does not economise.

SOMALIA

We are what we think.

NIGERIA

One who damages the character of another
damages his own.

YORUBA OF NIGERIA

Work on your reputation until it is established;
when it is established it will work for you.

TUNISIA

The house looks good from the outside,
but the inside is bad.

VAI OF LIBERIA

The child grows by medicine.

TSONGA OF SOUTH AFRICA, MOZAMBIQUE AND ZIMBABWE

Enjoy life before you have a child.

TIGRINYA OF ERITREA

Children always lead their parents into trouble.

TSWANA OF BOTSWANA AND SOUTH AFRICA

Give birth to children
and you'll be pregnant with worries.

NAMIBIA

Without children you are naked.

YORUBA OF NIGERIA

Children are the reward of life.

CONGOLESE

Don't rely on the river alone
to wean your child.

DINKA OF SUDAN

Crooked wood makes crooked ashes.

EWE OF WEST AFRICA

The way you bring up a child
is the way it grows up.

SWAHILI OF EAST AFRICA

He who was not taught by his mother
will be taught by the world.

SWAHILI OF EAST AFRICA

The child who provokes his mother
and father eats food without salt.

AKAN OF GHANA

A child who is to be successful
is not reared exclusively on a bed of down.

AKAN OF GHANA

There is no wealth
where there are not children.

LIBERIA

19

COMPLACENCY

The child who doesn't cry
dies in the blanket on its mother's back.

NDEBELE OF ZIMBABWE AND SOUTH AFRICA

He who waits for a chance
may wait for a long time.

YORUBA OF NIGERIA

That which passes, is allowed to pass.

SWAHILI OF EAST AFRICA

COMPLICITY

Live with him who prays, and thou prayest;
live with the singer, and thou singest.

EGYPT

One who keeps the company of a bad person,
becomes as bad.

MERU OF KENYA

Evil knows where evil sleeps.

NIGERIA

CONFIDENCE

Aiming isn't hitting.

SWAHILI OF EAST AFRICA

The eye crosses the river before the body.

NDEBELE OF ZIMBABWE AND SOUTH AFRICA

Having rain clouds is not the same as having rain.

KIKUYU OF KENYA

When the mouse laughs at the cat
there is a hole nearby.

NIGERIA

 ## CONFLICT

Two birds disputed over a kernel,
when a third swooped down and carried it off.

CONGOLESE

Don't stand up to a person
you can't defeat while sitting down.

SOMALIA

21

CONFLICT

Quarrels end, but words once spoken never die.

SIERRA LEONE

The solution to a conflict
is talking about the conflict.

SOMALIA

CONFORMITY

Copying everyone else all the time,
the monkey one day cut his throat.

ZULU OF SOUTH AFRICA

If you should find the residents of a place
frying their eyes, fry yours also.

NYANJA OF MALAWI AND ZAMBIA

Go the way that many people go;
if you go alone you will have reason to lament.

LOZI OF ZAMBIA, BOTSWANA AND ZIMBABWE

When a fowl arrives in a new town,
it stands on one leg until it knows that
it is a town where people stand on two legs.

NIGERIA

 CONSOLATION

Daylight follows a dark night.

MAASAI OF KENYA AND TANZANIA

Water does not stay in the sky forever.

KALENJIN OF KENYA

However long the night may last,
there will be morning.

MOROCCO

After distress, solace.

SWAHILI OF EAST AFRICA

CONVICTION

If you try to look too much into the eyes
of a dead body, you will see a ghost.

GHANA

Faith in God's generosity fills one's stomach.

SOMALIA

If you see someone riding a log,
compliment him on his beautiful horse.

TUNISIA

 ## COURAGE

Courage is the father of success.

NIGERIA

Who has more courage than a Maasai warrior?
answer: two Maasai warriors

MAASAI OF KENYA AND TANZANIA RIDDLE

24

If you even think of a rhino,
you must hide away.

TSWANA OF BOTSWANA AND SOUTH AFRICA

No one entrusts his mother to drunks.

KIRUNDI OF BURUNDI

If you see a quiet snake,
it is because it has swallowed another snake.

KIKUYU OF KENYA

He walks upon the highest part of the wall
and says, 'For safety we trust in God!'

EGYPT

If a bracelet fits wear it;
but if it hurts you,
throw it away no matter how shiny.

KENYA

Do not try to taste honey
if you see it on a thorn.

ETHIOPIA

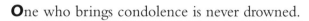

One who brings condolence is never drowned.

SOTHO OF SOUTH AFRICA,
meaning it is never too late to console the bereaved

Death is blind.

TSONGA OF SOUTH AFRICA, MOZAMBIQUE AND ZIMBABWE

The reward of life is death.

ANYUAK OF SUDAN

Death and laughter are brothers.

KALENJIN OF KENYA

Whatever you do you will die.

VAI OF LIBERIA

While you mark out a field,
death marks out your life.

OVIMBUNDU OF ANGOLA

Nobody knows which pot of beer will kill him.

RWANDA

DEBT

He who borrows sixty kobo and fails
to repay it loses the opportunity
of borrowing seventy kobo.

YORUBA OF NIGERIA

The mouth makes debts, but the arms repay.

EWE OF WEST AFRICA

Borrowing is the first-born of poverty.

FULA OF WEST AFRICA

DECEIT

The teeth are smiling, but is the heart?

CONGOLESE

Mrs Pleasant is up to no good;
if she's not a thief, she's a sorcerer.

VENDA OF SOUTH AFRICA

The person who shines a light on you by day
sets fire to you by night.

SWAHILI OF EAST AFRICA

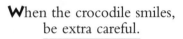

DECEIT

When the crocodile smiles,
be extra careful.

SWAHILI OF EAST AFRICA

 DESTINY

You may get up before dawn,
but destiny gets up before you.

KIRUNDI OF BURUNDI

No man's path lies in another's.

AKAN OF GHANA

Run as hard as a wild beast if you will,
but you won't get any reward greater
than that destined for you.

EGYPT

On the day a man is born his life is measured.

CHAGGA OF TANZANIA

What God has written cannot be erased.

SWAHILI OF EAST AFRICA

DISCRETION

No man should disclose another's origin.

AKAN OF GHANA

The discreet man knows how to hold his tongue.

MADAGASCAR

What the family talks about in the evening,
the child will talk about in the morning.

OROMO OF ETHIOPIA AND KENYA

ENMITY

A powerful friend becomes a powerful enemy.

ETHIOPIA

An intelligent enemy
is better than a stupid friend.

SENEGAL

An enemy slaughters, a friend distributes.

FULA OF WEST AFRICA

29

EQUALITY

The only equals are those who are equally rich.

KIRUNDI OF BURUNDI

ETHNICITY

A race is as fragile as a newborn child.

CONGOLESE

A clan is like a flowering shrub,
it blossoms in clusters.

AKAN OF GHANA

The elephant never gets tired
of carrying his tusks.

VAI OF LIBERIA

Where your ancestors do not live,
you cannot build your house.

KONGO OF ANGOLA

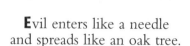

Evil enters like a needle
and spreads like an oak tree.

ETHIOPIA

Be it wickedness or be it goodness,
neither goes unrequited.

YORUBA OF NIGERIA

If there were no retaliation,
there would be no evil.

NIGERIA

 EXILE

From the day I left my country
I cannot laugh with my teeth.

MOROCCO

The goat is not big in cowtown.

VAI OF LIBERIA

The tar of my country is better
than the honey of other countries.

MOROCCO

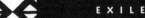

EXILE

My country is my country,
even though it is unjust to me.

MOROCCO

FAMILY

As an ox is not overburdened with its horns,
so a family is not overburdened with a member.

OROMO OF KENYA AND ETHIOPIA

Dine with a stranger,
but save your love for your family.

ETHIOPIA

The family is like the forest;
if you are outside it looks dense,
if you are inside you see that
each tree has its own position.

AKAN OF GHANA

None but a mule deserves his family.

MOROCCO

FEAR

The dog's bark is not might, but fright.

MADAGASCAR

One who enters the forest does not turn back when hearing twigs breaking in the brush.

BEMBA OF ZAMBIA

FIDELITY

If you want sex while travelling, travel with your wife.

MINYANKA OF MALI

If you marry a woman you meet on the dance floor, one day she'll run off with the drummer.

YORUBA OF NIGERIA

A tender bamboo shoot should not be desired for building a hut.

CHEWA OF MALAWI

Married women are like elephants' tusks: don't touch them.

SWAHILI OF EAST AFRICA

The lizard dropped from the top of the coconut
tree, and, nodding his head up and down,
asked the earth if it felt dizzy.

AKAN OF GHANA

He is a fool whose sheep runs away twice.

AKAN OF GHANA

A fool looks for dung
where the cow never browsed.

ETHIOPIA

Everybody loves a fool,
but nobody wants him for a son.

MALINKE OF MALI

The fool is thirsty in the midst of water.

OROMO OF ETHIOPIA AND KENYA

By the time the fool has learned the game,
the players have dispersed.

AKAN OF GHANA

He who forgives gains the victory.

YORUBA OF NIGERIA

A bitter heart devours its owner.

TSWANA OF BOTSWANA AND HERERO OF NAMIBIA

 FRIENDSHIP

There is no better mirror than an old friend.

CAPE VERDE

The stomach creates friendships.

MAASAI OF KENYA AND TANZANIA

Hold a true friend with both your hands.

NIGERIA

When you know who his friend is,
you know who he is.

SENEGAL

FUTILITY

You cannot turn the wind, so turn the sail.

SWAHILI OF EAST AFRICA

You cannot make powder
by pounding water with mortar and pestle.

MERU OF KENYA

If you are on the road to nowhere,
find another road.

AKAN OF GHANA

A sinking vessel needs no navigation.

SWAHILI OF EAST AFRICA

 GARRULOUSNESS

He who talks incessantly talks nonsense.

CÔTE D'IVOIRE

A chattering bird builds no nest.

DUALA OF CAMEROON

When the heart overflows,
it comes out through the mouth.

ETHIOPIA

GENEROSITY

The best generosity is that which is quick.

EGYPT

One does not give a gift without a motive.

MALI

One 'I give you' is worth more
than one 'I love you.'

RWANDA

To give to him that gave to you
is not giving, it is repaying.

SWAHILI OF EAST AFRICA

The turtledove doesn't say 'Give! Give!'
but 'Give to him who gives to you!'

KIRUNDI OF BURUNDI

May God free you,
then the doctors may boast.

OVIMBUNDU OF ANGOLA

Every knot has an unraveller in God.

EGYPT

No one teaches a child God.

AKAN OF GHANA

If you wish to say something to God,
tell it to the wind.

AKAN OF GHANA,
meaning God is everywhere and accessible

Give thanks to God
if you live long enough to grow old.

RWANDA

GOODNESS

Greenness is never wholly absent
from the woods and goodness
is never wholly absent from people.

OVIMBUNDU OF ANGOLA

A good man earns more than his wages.

ETHIOPIA

Good is when I steal other people's wives
and cattle; bad is when they steal mine.

KHOISAN OF SOUTHERN AFRICA

GRATITUDE

If God did not give
the remarkable swallow anything,
at least he endowed it
with swiftness in turning.

AKAN OF GHANA

A dog goes where it is given bread.

ACHOLI OF UGANDA

39

Don't blame God for having created
the tiger, but give him thanks
for not having given the tiger wings.

AMHARIC OF ETHIOPIA

The frog says,
'Although I have nothing,
I always have my hop!'

VAI OF LIBERIA

 GREED

A leech that doesn't let go even when full,
dies on the dry land.

NIGERIA

Thou kissest thy lover,
and tearest out his teeth.

EGYPT

Those carrying an elephant home
on their heads, need not dig up crickets
with their toes on the way.

NIGERIA

 GUILT

He who is guilty is the one that has much to say.

AKAN OF GHANA

If there were no fault,
there would be no pardon.

EGYPT

The person found guilty in a trial,
will boast that he will press the case further.

NIGERIA

 HAPPINESS

If you don't laugh at Christmas
you'll not be happy for the rest of your life.

ETHIOPIAN BELIEF

To be happy in one's home
is better than to be a chief.

YORUBA OF NIGERIA

Anticipate the good so that you may enjoy it.

ETHIOPIA

A beast that is passing finishes no grass.

ZULU OF SOUTH AFRICA

Don't be in a hurry to swallow
when chewing is pleasant.

NYANJA OF MALAWI AND ZAMBIA

It is not rushing that is important;
it is making sure.

MAASAI OF KENYA AND TANZANIA

Mr Run-to-get-warm left the fire
as it was beginning to blaze.

NYANJA OF MALAWI AND ZAMBIA

Clothes put on while running,
come off while running.

ETHIOPIA

Do not rush while your clothes are still tangled.

MAASAI OF KENYA AND TANZANIA

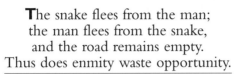

The snake flees from the man;
the man flees from the snake,
and the road remains empty.
Thus does enmity waste opportunity.

 OROMO OF ETHIOPIA AND KENYA

He who hates, hates himself.

ZULU OF SOUTH AFRICA

Don't try to make someone hate
the person he loves, for he will still go on loving,
but he will hate you.

SENEGAL

Hate has no medicine.

GHANA

HEALTH

The head and the body must serve each other.

WOLOF OF SENEGAL AND THE GAMBIA

Sickness accompanies a waning moon;
a new moon cures disease.

SOTHO OF LESOTHO AND SOUTH AFRICA BELIEF

HOPE

Hope is the pillar of the world.

KANURI OF NIGERIA AND NIGER

What one hopes for is always better
than what one has.

ETHIOPIA

The whole world burns
but a little patch could survive.

MAASAI OF KENYA AND TANZANIA

The foot has no nose.

XHOSA OF SOUTH AFRICA,
meaning that you should be hospitable because you don't know where
you might go in the future, and require hospitality yourself

The stomach of a guest is smaller than the horn of a goat.

ZIMBABWE

God bless him who pays visits, and short visits.

EGYPT

Let the guests arrive, that we may be satisfied.

DINKA OF SUDAN

The day we came we ate off dishes, now we are eating out of wooden bowls.

OVIMBUNDU OF ANGOLA

A guest has the poise of a gentleman, and the eye of a detective.

SOMALIA

45

A person is a person through other persons.

ZULU OF SOUTH AFRICA

Trees never meet (but people do).

NAMIBIA

It is people who make the world;
the bush has wounds and scars.

MALAWI

We and the cows are all the same;
we drink the same milk.

FULA OF WEST AFRICA

Man is the worst animal there is.

UGANDA

The stranger with his belly full
of good food runs to a woman,
while you with only a scrap of wood to gnaw
must drag along your saucepan.

MAASAI OF KENYA AND TANZANIA

A person without food is a sure slave.

TONGA OF ZAMBIA

Today's hunger does not share itself
with tomorrow's hunger.

BAMBARA OF MALI

When hunger gets inside you,
nothing else can.

YORUBA OF NIGERIA

There is no God like one's stomach:
We must sacrifice to it everyday.

YORUBA OF NIGERIA

47

There is no wormwood that comes into flower
and does not wither.

ZULU OF SOUTH AFRICA

When a thing becomes perfect it soon fades.

MOROCCO

Even though the old man is strong and hearty,
he will not live forever.

AKAN OF GHANA

When a man or a reed dies another springs up.

NYANJA OF MALAWI AND ZAMBIA

Little and lasting is better
than much and passing.

MOROCCO

When the mouth is small
the beard gets the crumbs.

EWE OF WEST AFRICA

The frog wanted to be
as big as the elephant, and burst.

ETHIOPIA

Because he has so many trades,
he is unemployed.

TUNISIA

He who's unable to dance
says the yard is stony.

KENYA

He who can do nothing,
does nothing.

WOLOF OF SENEGAL AND THE GAMBIA

Two bulls cannot stay in the same kraal.

TSWANA OF BOTSWANA AND SOUTH AFRICA

His opinions are like water
in the bottom of a canoe,
going from side to side.

EFIK OF NIGERIA

He who hunts two rats, catches none.

BAGANDA OF UGANDA

Two lucrative paths made the hyena indecisive.

ABALUYIA OF KENYA

A paddle here, a paddle there –
the canoe stays still.

SIERRA LEONE

You can borrow a basket and a sieve;
you cannot borrow a face.

OVIMBUNDU OF ANGOLA

The elephant is one thing and the worm another.

AKAN OF GHANA

Nobody walks with another man's gait.

KIKUYU OF KENYA

A hare is like an ass in the length of its ears,
yet it is not its son.

BAMBARA OF MALI

Can you tie two penises in a knot?

ACHOLI OF UGANDA; *referring to the belief that men
fight and compete with each other to assert their individuality*

When wood breaks, it can be repaired.
But ivory breaks forever.

YORUBA OF NIGERIA

INDUSTRIOUSNESS

Only early risers see unusual things.

TSWANA OF BOTSWANA AND SOUTH AFRICA

He who has harvested in time of famine
will always find a wife.

KIRUNDI OF BURUNDI

The cow is helped which helps itself.

SOTHO OF LESOTHO AND SOUTH AFRICA

He who rises early skips in the dew.

KIKUYU OF KENYA

 INGRATITUDE

I pointed out the stars and the moon,
and all you saw was the tip of my finger.

SWAHILI OF EAST AFRICA

Let the skirt waste
if I don't get it for New Year.

ETHIOPIA

52

He gets his passage for nothing,
and winks to the wife of the captain of the ship.

EGYPT

Ingratitude is sooner or later fatal to its author.

AKAN OF GHANA

If I had lighted for thee my ten fingers
to use as candles thou would still regard them
as if they were in darkness.

EGYPT

I put a date in his mouth,
and he puts a stick in my eye!

TUNISIA

 INTELLIGENCE

Beauty is half a God-given favour;
intelligence a whole one.

FULA OF WEST AFRICA

He who does not know one thing,
knows another.

KIKUYU OF KENYA

53

INTELLIGENCE

Knowledge is better than riches.

CAMEROON

INTIMACY

You can take the lid off a pot to see
what is inside; a person has no lid.

VENDA OF SOUTH AFRICA,
meaning you cannot read a person's heart

Eyes which have met
have established a relationship.

SHONA OF ZIMBABWE AND MOZAMBIQUE

Only when you have crossed the river
can you say the crocodile has a lump on his snout.

AKAN OF GHANA

It is the wife who knows her husband.

AKAN OF GHANA

A thousand raps at the door,
but no salute or invitation from within.

EGYPT

Do not call a person a witch
before he has bewitched you.

KALENJIN OF KENYA

The bad neighbour sees only what enters
the house, not what goes from it.

EGYPT

Don't sweep someone else's house
while yours is dirty.

MAASAI OF KENYA AND TANZANIA

A good house is not judged by its door.

SWAHILI OF EAST AFRICA

We shall not hate the hated
until we sleep in their house.

KALENJIN OF KENYA

The walls of the house don't tell you
what's going on inside.

RWANDA

55

JUSTICE

Justice is like fire;
even if one covers it with a veil, it still burns.

MADAGASCAR

Equality in injustice is justice.

EGYPT

In a court of fowls,
the cockroach never wins his case.

RWANDA

KINDNESS

A kind person is the one who is kind to strangers.

KONGO OF THE DEMOCRATIC REPUBLIC OF THE CONGO

The food of a woman who speaks sweetly
will never be rejected by her husband.

IGBO OF NIGERIA

God gives nothing to those
who keep their arms crossed.

BAMBARA OF MALI

The desires of the lazy
are too great for their labours.

BAMBARA OF MALI

The lazy one is pregnant in the sowing season.

KIRUNDI OF BURUNDI

If stretching were wealth,
the cat would be rich.

GHANA

Who comes last drinks muddy water.

ACHOLI OF UGANDA

A chief is a tree on which all birds sit.

SOTHO OF LESOTHO AND SOUTH AFRICA

A chief is a chief by virtue of his people.

TSWANA OF BOTSWANA AND SOUTH AFRICA

To love the king is not bad,
but a king who loves you is better.

WOLOF OF SENEGAL AND THE GAMBIA

The tyrant is only the slave turned inside out.

EGYPT

Chief you kill me with laughter.

ACHOLI OF UGANDA,
expression used to criticise those who kowtow to leaders

Too many captains sink the ship.

TUNISIA

 LEARNING

Instruction in youth is like engraving in stone.

BERBER OF NORTH AFRICA

Knowledge is like a garden:
if it is not cultivated, it cannot be harvested.

GUINEA

Acquire learning and information
even if they come from the mouth of cows.

EGYPT

The habit of thinking
is the habit of gaining strength.

NIGERIA

 LIFE

Life is a loom on which God holds the threads.

BERBER OF NORTH AFRICA

One day is in favour of you,
and another day against you.

MOROCCO

LIFE

The race of life is never tiresome.

<small>IGBO OF NIGERIA</small>

There are many dawns.

<small>TSWANA OF BOTSWANA AND SOUTH AFRICA</small>

LOVE

On the way to one's beloved there are no hills.

<small>KIKUYU OF KENYA</small>

Let your love be like the misty rains,
coming softly, but flooding the river.

<small>MADAGASCAR</small>

Love is a donkey freed of all tethers.

<small>FULA OF WEST AFRICA</small>

Don't love me as you do a door,
pushed to and fro.

<small>MADAGASCAR</small>

For news of the heart, ask the face.

HAUSA OF NIGER AND NIGERIA

Love is like a baby; it needs to be treated gently.

CONGOLESE

Love is like a rice plant; transplanted,
it can grow elsewhere.

MADAGASCAR

To love someone who does not love you
is like shaking a tree to make the dew drops fall.

CONGOLESE

You know whom you love;
you cannot know who loves you.

YORUBA OF NIGERIA

A hearty eater is not in love.

ETHIOPIA

Hearts do not meet one another like roads.

KENYA

LUCK

Throw him into the river
and he will rise with a fish in his mouth.

EGYPT

It's better to be lucky than to be good.

LUO OF KENYA

Luck goes where luck is.

ABALUYIA OF KENYA

A rose fell to the lot of the monkey.

EGYPTIAN,
expression for those who are believed to be undeserving of their good luck

Good fortune does not roar as it comes.

MAASAI OF KENYA AND TANZANIA

One falsehood spoils a thousand truths.

AKAN OF GHANA

Lies do not make one wealthy.

SOTHO OF LESOTHO AND SOUTH AFRICA

Tell little, little lies — as tiny as needles.
When they get as big as a hoe,
they will strike you dead.

YORUBA OF NIGERIA

Rather than tell a lie to help a friend,
assist him to pay the fine for his offence.

NIGERIA

To lie about a far country is easy.

ETHIOPIA

If a person stands up
and his clothes stick between his buttocks,
it means he is in the habit of telling lies.

SWAHILI OF EAST AFRICA BELIEF

Marriage without good faith
is like a teapot without a tray.

MOROCCO

The man who says he will not marry a woman
with other admirers, will not marry a woman.

YORUBA OF NIGERIA

Hasty marriages bring hasty divorces.

OROMO OF ETHIOPIA AND KENYA

A woman who has not been married twice
cannot know perfect marriage.

YORUBA OF NIGERIA

One who eats straight from the cooking pot
will have heavy rain on his wedding day.

SWAHILI OF EAST AFRICA BELIEF

If a girl refuses marriage,
just wait for her breasts to sag.

KIRUNDI OF BURUNDI

MATERIALISM

Cattle are the nation; if they die the nation dies.

XHOSA OF SOUTH AFRICA

You are beautiful because of your possessions.

BAGIRMI OF CHAD

Luxury begins the day a man starts wearing shoes.

TUAREG OF WEST AFRICA

 MONEY

Money can make people laugh,
but when they laugh, the foolish ones
sometimes forget to close their mouths.

NIGERIA

Money kills more people than a club.

NUPE OF NIGERIA

Love, pain and money cannot be kept secret;
they soon betray themselves.

SENEGAL

Profit is profit even in Mecca.

HAUSA OF NIGER AND NIGERIA

Abundance of money is a trial for a man.

MOROCCO

You put the yam to bed in the ground
it will bring you money that will plant you
on top of a beautiful woman.

YORUBA OF NIGERIA SAYING

The midwife can't take the baby for her pay.

VAI OF LIBERIA; *expression for unrealistic compensation requests*

If you feel an itching on your right palm
it means that you will receive money.
If you feel an itching on your left palm
it means you will spend money.

SWAHILI OF EAST AFRICA BELIEF

To embrace a child is to embrace its mother.

Sotho of Lesotho and South Africa

When you stand with the blessings
of your mother and God,
it matters not who stands against you.

Yoruba of Nigeria

A mother lying down
sees farther than a child in a tree.

Krio of Sierra Leone

A mother's tears are no hard work.

Mongo of the Democratic Republic of the Congo

A woman whose sons have died
is richer than a barren woman.

Kikuyu of Kenya

No man will starve in his mother's house.

Liberia

It is not only one mother
who can cook a nice soup.

GA OF GHANA AND EFIK OF NIGERIA

Everyone is in the hands of his mother.

BAMBARA OF MALI

He who takes anything to his mother
never says it is too heavy.

BAGANDA OF UGANDA

 MYSTERY

The deeds of God and the smile of a dog,
one does not understand.

OROMO OF ETHIOPIA AND KENYA

A thing without end is mysterious.

SHONA OF ZIMBABWE AND MOZAMBIQUE

Small boys and smoke disappear mysteriously.

ETHIOPIA

NATURE

The world was not given to you by your parents,
it was lent to you by your children.

KENYA

To look at green adorns the heart and the eye.

MOROCCO

The forest is everything.

PYGMY OF CENTRAL AFRICA

 NEGOTIATION

He who has warned you
has not killed you yet.

SOMALIA

Where there is negotiation,
there is hope for agreement.

SOMALIA

When the bag tears, the shoulders get a rest.

AKAN OF GHANA

While the sun is shining, bask!
(Tomorrow there may be clouds.)

NYANJA OF MALAWI AND ZAMBIA

When you eat crow, call it pigeon.

ETHIOPIA

The traveller's path is marked by the stars,
not the sand dunes.

NILOTIC

The news of the evening
may triumph over that of the morning.

MAASAI OF KENYA AND TANZANIA

A string may make it possible to wait for a rope.

MAASAI OF KENYA AND TANZANIA

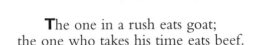

The one in a rush eats goat;
the one who takes his time eats beef.

SOTHO OF LESÒTHO AND SOUTH AFRICA

Do not hurry the night,
the sun will always rise for its own sake.

ERITREA

It is patience which gets you out of the net.

NYANJA OF MALAWI AND ZAMBIA

If one is not in a hurry,
even an egg will start walking.

ETHIOPIA

 PEACE

Silence produces peace, and peace produces safety.

SWAHILI OF EAST AFRICA

Peace is costly, but it is worth the expense.

KIKUYU OF KENYA

71

The perseverance of the river
turned it into an ocean.

SHONA OF ZIMBABWE AND MOZAMBIQUE

By trying repeatedly,
the monkey learns to jump from the tree.

CAMEROON

Little by little,
the tortoise arrived at the Indian Ocean.

NYANJA OF MALAWI AND ZAMBIA

People are like plants in the wind:
they bow down and rise up again.

MADAGASCAR

By going and coming,
a bird weaves its nest.

AKAN OF GHANA

Standing is still going.

SWAHILI OF EAST AFRICA

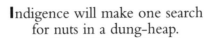

Indigence will make one search
for nuts in a dung-heap.

AKAN OF GHANA

If Europe knew no poverty,
the white man would not leave his people
to live in the black man's country.

AKAN OF GHANA

Poverty is like madness
(in what it makes you do).

AKAN OF GHANA

 POWER

Even an elephant can be eaten by small insects.

NDEBELE OF ZIMBABWE AND SOUTH AFRICA

Power is like holding an egg in the hand;
if you hold it too tightly it breaks,
and if you hold it too loosely, it drops.

AKAN OF GHANA

POWER

Frowning frogs cannot stop the cows
drinking from the pool.

KIKUYU OF KENYA

No one following an elephant
needs to knock the dew off the grass.

AKAN OF GHANA

A man of power may be right or wrong,
but he is always right.

BAMBARA OF MALI

PREPAREDNESS

A person does not begin to forge a gun
when the war has already arrived in the village.

NYANJA OF MALAWI AND ZAMBIA

You cannot build a house for last winter.

ETHIOPIA

You cannot shave a man's head in his absence.

NIGER

May God preserve us from
'If I had only known!'

HAUSA OF NIGER AND NIGERIA

Before shooting, one must aim.

NIGERIA

Before eating, open your mouth.

WOLOF OF SENEGAL AND THE GAMBIA

PRIDE

Pride only goes the length one can spit.

CONGOLESE

To crawl on one's hands and knees
has never prevented one from walking upright.

MERU OF KENYA

In the eyes of its mother,
every beetle is a gazelle.

MOROCCO

A man who lives by the Niger
does not wash himself in spittle.

NIGER

The heart is like a tree,
it grows where it wishes.

SHONA OF ZIMBABWE AND MOZAMBIQUE

What is sensible today
may be madness another time.

YORUBA OF NIGERIA

Don't be so much in love
that you can't tell when the rain comes.

MADAGASCAR

76

The one-eyed person is a beauty
in the country of the blind.

EGYPT

The mist of the coast is the rain upland.

OVIMBUNDU OF ANGOLA

If there were no elephant in the jungle,
the buffalo would be a great animal.

GHANA

The mouse in his hole is king.

BERBER OF NORTH AFRICA

RELIABILITY

A floating log never becomes a crocodile.

SONGHAI OF NIGER

No matter how much the world degenerates,
one will never find worms in salt.

NIGERIA

77

The young cannot teach tradition to the old.

YORUBA OF NIGERIA

If you never offer palm wine to your uncle,
you will not learn any proverbs.

YORUBA OF NIGERIA

No man can be blessed
without the acceptance of his own head.

YORUBA OF NIGERIA

 RESPONSIBILITY

He who bites gets bitten.

ZULU OF SOUTH AFRICA

If farmers do not cultivate their fields,
the people in the town will die of hunger.

GUINEA

He who is scared of a hyena's howling,
is he who has smeared himself with fat.

SHONA OF ZIMBABWE AND MOZAMBIQUE

Do not look where you fell,
but where you slipped.

VAI OF LIBERIA

If a child has sinned all have sinned.

KIKUYU OF KENYA

SECRETS

A secret is no secret when shared by two people.

SWAHILI OF EAST AFRICA

A wise man talks about secrets only to his heart.

SWAHILI OF EAST AFRICA

SHAME

Where there is no shame, there is no honour.

CONGOLESE

Better to blush
than keep the burden in your heart.

TUNISIA

79

SILENCE

Silence is the door of consent.

BERBER OF NORTH AFRICA

Not to talk is to hate.

KIKUYU OF KENYA

Silence is also a form of speech.

FULA OF WEST AFRICA

SOLIDARITY

If you are at peace, so am I,
but if you are in trouble so am I.

SHONA OF ZIMBABWE AND MOZAMBIQUE

A single bracelet does not jingle.

CONGOLESE

When minds are the same,
that which is far off will come.

EAST AFRICA

When spider webs unite, they can tie up a lion.

ETHIOPIA

Sticks in a bundle are unbreakable.

BONDEI OF TANZANIA

SORROW

Elegy is the voice of the survivor.

SOMALIA

Sorrow is like a precious treasure
shown only to friends.

MADAGASCAR

SPEECH

Words are like bullets;
once escaped, you can't catch them again.

WOLOF OF SENEGAL AND THE GAMBIA

The fool and a rich man
can say what they please.

ETHIOPIA

The tree remembers,
the axe does not remember.

SHONA OF ZIMBABWE AND MOZAMBIQUE

Great events may stem
from words of no importance.

CONGOLESE

The wound caused by words
is worse than the wound of bodies.

MOROCCO

The speech of a man which is beautiful
and understood is better than the speech
of a thousand mouths that is not.

MOROCCO

Words are sweet,
but they never take the place of food.

IGBO OF NIGERIA

A healthy ear can stand hearing sick words.

SENEGAL

THEFT

A stolen object does not fill one's heart with joy.

MONGO OF THE DEMOCRATIC REPUBLIC OF CONGO

There is no difference
between the thief and the looker-on.

KIKUYU OF KENYA

THOUGHTLESSNESS

Laugh at the madman
only when you have stopped bearing children.

SHONA OF ZIMBABWE AND MOZAMBIQUE

The log in the pile
laughs at the log already in the fire.

KIKUYU, MAASAI AND KALENJIN OF KENYA

The one being carried
does not realise how far away the town is.

NIGERIA

The man who has bread to eat
does not appreciate the severity of a famine.

YORUBA OF NIGERIA

83

A son who never leaves home
will always think his mother's is the loudest fart.

KIKUYU OF KENYA

Eyes that have beheld the ocean
can no longer be afraid of the lagoon.

YORUBA OF NIGERIA

If you want to understand somebody,
go with him on a journey.

ABALUYIA OF KENYA

Travelling teaches men their way.

KIKUYU OF KENYA

Rather hear the flatulencies of camels,
than the prayers of the fishes.

EGYPT,
expression for those who prefer to travel by land than by sea

One who does not travel
will not know the value of men.

MOROCCO

He who travels surpasses his mother in wisdom.

ABALUYIA OF KENYA

Truth and morning become light with time.

ETHIOPIA

The neck of truth cannot be broken.

MAASAI OF KENYA AND TANZANIA

The hatching of an egg is unpleasant for the shell.

KANURI OF NIGERIA AND NIGER

Only the eyes tell the truth,
not the stories one hears.

KUBA OF THE DEMOCRATIC REPUBLIC OF THE CONGO

He who tells the truth is not well liked.

BAMBARA OF MALI

Bitter truth is better than sweet lies.

SWAHILI OF EAST AFRICA

Who tells the truth is never wrong.

SWAHILI OF EAST AFRICA

85

An enemy defeated by truth
will never return,
but an enemy defeated by weapon
is certain to return.

KENYA

War has no eyes.

SWAHILI OF EAST AFRICA

War and drought, peace and milk.

SOMALIA

Where elephants fight,
it is the reeds that get hurt.

SWAHILI OF EAST AFRICA

It is they who have not died in war that start it.

KIKUYU OF KENYA

After the hyena passes, the dog barks.

ETHIOPIA

If the state is going to fall
it is from the belly.

AKAN OF GHANA

The destroyer of a country
is the son of the country.

SWAHILI OF EAST AFRICA

The least valuable among men
is the one who would rather inwardly
eat himself up rather than state his case.

SOMALIA

Hit him with a bean he will break.

TUNISIAN EXPRESSION FOR A WEAK PERSON

87

He who is troubled by having property
is better off than he who is troubled by poverty.

KIKUYU OF KENYA

Superabundance is not far from want.

NIGERIA

Wealth is like hair in the nose;
if much is pulled out, it is painful,
if little, it is painful.

MADAGASCAR

Wealth that takes only one market week to
acquire is sure to contain within it things for
which the gods will surely make claims.

NIGERIA

One does not cook one's nobility and eat;
it is wealth that counts.

AKAN OF GHANA

Blessings are better than wealth.

SWAHILI OF EAST AFRICA

When a rich man gets drunk,
you say he is indisposed.

AKAN OF GHANA

 WISDOM

Wisdom is not bought.

AKAN OF GHANA

The heart of a wise man
lies quiet like limpid water.

CAMEROON

Not even God is wise enough.

YORUBA OF NIGERIA

You do not teach the paths of the forest
to an old gorilla.

CONGOLESE

89

Wisdom is not like money
to be tied up and hidden.

AKAN OF GHANA

The one who listens to the voice of the elderly
is strong like a tree, the one who turns
a deaf ear is like a twig in the wind.

NILOTIC

The old woman has a reason
for running in the rice field.

BAULE OF CÔTE D'IVOIRE

Misfortune will befall one
who plays the fool with old people.

XHOSA OF SOUTH AFRICA

Wisdom is pieced together.

AKAN OF GHANA

The pillow imparts wisdom.

GHANA

The words of one's elders
are greater than an amulet.

AKAN OF GHANA

Just because a child has as many clothes
as his father, doesn't mean he has worn out
as many clothes as his father.

YORUBA OF NIGERIA

An old he goat does not sneeze for nothing.

KIKUYU OF KENYA

 WIVES

With one wife the heart is warmed;
with the other wife the kettle is warmed.

OROMO OF ETHIOPIA AND KENYA

A good wife is her husband's crown.

ETHIOPIA

A wife is like a blanket;
when you cover yourself with it,
it irritates you,
yet if you cast it aside,
you feel cold.

AKAN OF GHANA

The man may be the head of the home;
the wife is the heart.

KIKUYU OF KENYA

Two wives, two pots of poison.

KIKUYU OF KENYA

It is better to have a disorderly wife
than to remain a bachelor.

EWE OF WEST AFRICA

WOMEN

Woman and the sky cannot be understood.

KIKUYU OF KENYA

The stick of a girl is
'touch-me-and-I-am-gone.'

RWANDA

A woman you love for her being,
not for her beauty.

SWAHILI OF EAST AFRICA

WORK

Work is the medicine for poverty.

YORUBA OF NIGERIA

The ox eats hay,
the dog eats bread,
while the donkey that carries wine
drinks water.

OROMO OF ETHIOPIA AND KENYA

The jaws have nothing to chew
if the feet do not walk.

BAKUSU OF THE DEMOCRATIC REPUBLIC OF THE CONGO

Working in the fields is hard,
but hunger is harder.

NILOTIC